VANCE
THE CREDIT DOCTOR

ISBN : 979-8-218-18613-5 Paperback

Design: www.helenbarriosbooks.com

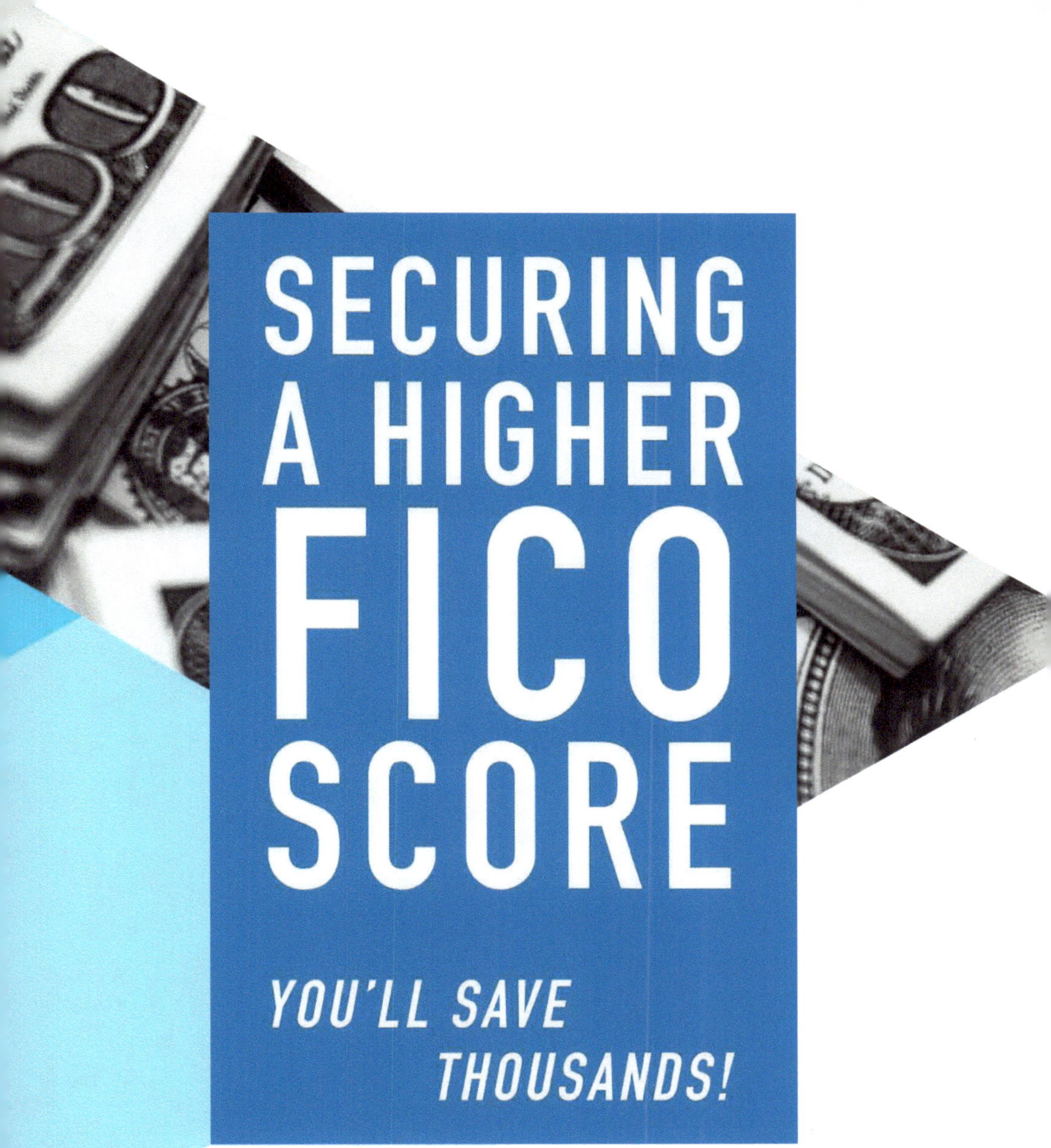

SECURING A HIGHER FICO SCORE

YOU'LL SAVE THOUSANDS!

Vance Dotson

TABLE OF CONTENT

What is a secured credit card?

If you deposit $2,000 into a bank account and then apply for a secured credit card with a $2,000 limit from that bank, the card is secured because the bank has the collateral it needs, which is the money. A secured credit card is an extremely helpful tool for rebuilding your FICO scores.

What are the benefits of the secured card?

1. Increases your fico scores

2. Increases your High Credit Limit

Availability:

$2,000

3. Decreases your debt to credit ratio

4. Attracts bigger future credit card offers

No Active Credit Cards

Go to a local credit union and obtain a secured credit card.

Questions you should ask the Credit Union

- Does your credit union offer the secured card program?
- How often can I increase the secured credit card amount?

  (That is the most important part of the secured credit card) If you can't increase it, you want to go to another credit union.
- What limit can I increase the Secured card to?

  (Most credit unions offer up to $25,000. Ask three credit unions and go with the one that offers the highest limit. The reason being if a credit union only offers a $5,000 secured card, you might need more than $5,000 to achieve your goals).

How should I use the secured credit card?

While building your FICO scores you should NEVER use the secured credit card.

How do I keep activity on the secured credit card?

If you use the secured credit card at a local gas station, yes that's an activity. However, it's detrimental to building a FICO score. The proper way to keep the last date of activity current is by increasing the secured credit card and increasing it often.

WRONG **WRONG** **WRONG**

Typically, when some consumers start with a secured credit card, it's usually a few hundred dollars so using the card for purchases would be detrimental to your debt to credit ratio.

How often should I increase the secured credit card?

MONTHLY - BIWEEKLY - WEEKLY - DAILY

Increase your secured credit card amount as often as possible. Remember, it's your money and you have total control. You can increase it every day, every week, bi-weekly or monthly. The thing is the more the better. Increasing the secured credit card is positive ACTIVITY.

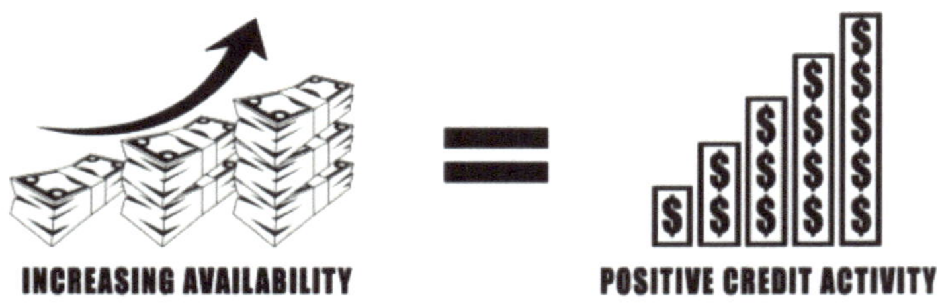

‘BIG FISH EATS LITTLE FISH’

In the city of Oklahoma City, Bob is known for catching big fish but no one could figure out how. On Saturday mornings, Bob would go to the local bait shop and purchase night crawlers. Bob had a few fishing poles. The first fishing pole has a small hook designed for the night crawlers which primarily catches small fish.

The other two poles have a bigger hook and are designed for bigger bait. Bob would catch small fish with the first pole and use the small fish as bait to put on the two bigger poles. The two bigger poles would catch much bigger fish from the small fish.

The moral of the story is the more you put down on the secured credit card in the beginning, the more it is worth to you.

Banks make money by lending money!

What does this mean for you? The more you can invest in yourself with the secured credit card, the bigger higher credit limits will come your way, the more your debt to credit percentages will go down, and the more your FICO scores will increase.

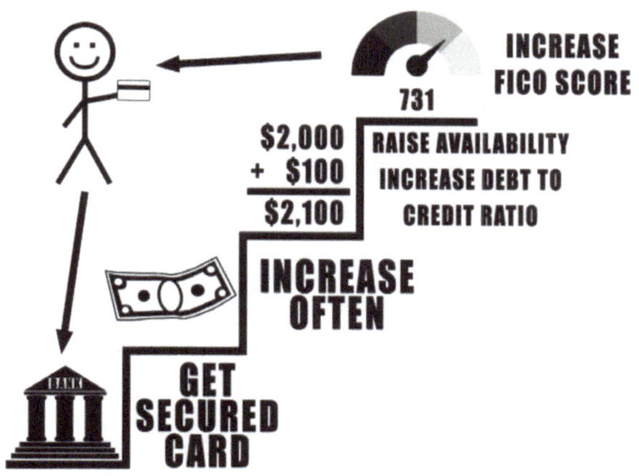

Key points, no doubt a higher FICO score will save you money.

If you're in the area of buying a home or car it's highly suggested that you raise your FICO score before contacting a realtor or credit union for financing for a home or a car.

For this example, if you're a few points shy from the next lending tier this method will save you money (thousands). For a mortgage, increasing your FICO scores by 40-50 points saves you over $100,000 in interest over the life of the loan. On an average car deal it can save you over $15,000 over the life of the loan.

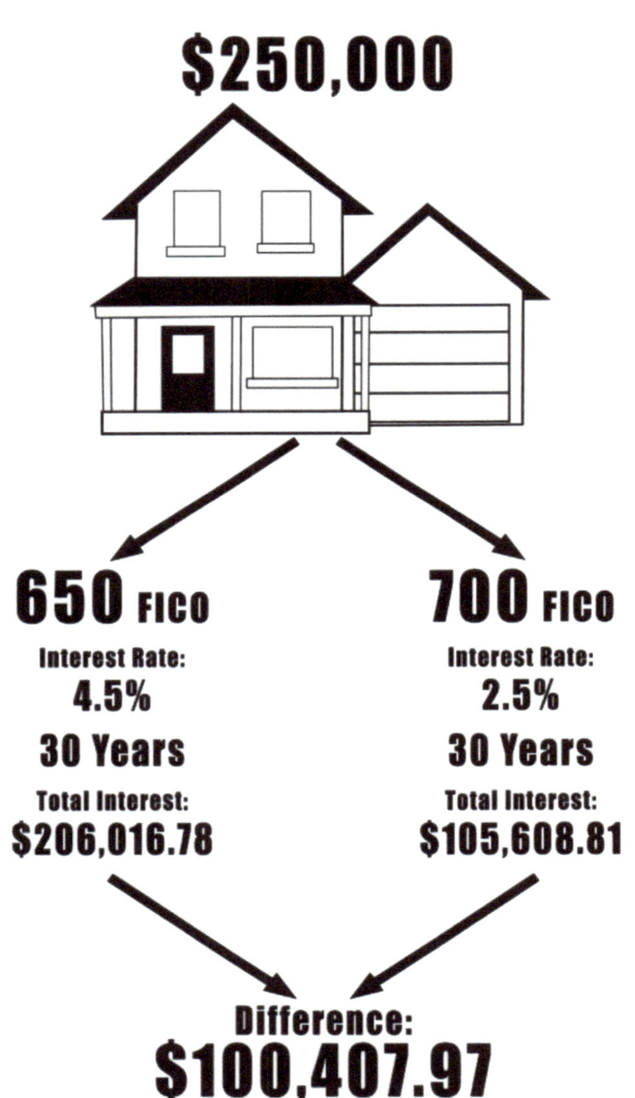
$250,000
650 FICO
Interest Rate:
4.5%
30 Years
Total Interest:
$206,016.78
700 FICO
Interest Rate:
2.5%
30 Years
Total Interest:
$105,608.81
Difference:
$100,407.97

How much money do you make each year?
Ask yourself how much longer you would have to work just to pay off the interest that you are paying on essential items.

SECRET
THE MORE YOU INVEST IN YOURSELF THE EASIER THE PROCESS IS

When do I get my money back?

Assuming you've obtained at least $5,000 and up unsecured credit cards requesting your money back from the local credit union would be fine. Remember banks make money by lending money and credit card companies/banks want you to use their products. The ultimate goal here is to attract as many credit card offers as possible.

INVEST IN YOURSELF!

'If you are willing to do the work
you can have anything.'

Information from www.MyFico.com

What is Amounts Owed?

In a very general sense, Amounts owed refers to how much debt you carry in total. However, the amount of debt you have is not as significant to your credit score as your credit utilization. When a high percentage of a person's available credit is been used, this can indicate that a person is overextended, and is more likely to make late or missed payments.

Amounts owed on accounts determines 30% of a FICO®Score

FICO research has found that your level of debt is predictive of future credit performance because the amount owed typically impacts your ability to pay all monthly credit obligations on time.

Not to worry if you have debt — it doesn't automatically make you a high-risk borrower. However, as your balances increase so does the probability of difficulty meeting monthly payments on time, but that's just part of what determines your credit score.

Part of the science of scoring is determining how much is too much for a given credit profile. Your FICO Scores take into account several factors.

There are 5 factors that the Amounts Owed Category looks at.

The amount owed on all accounts

Note that even if you pay off your credit cards in full each month, your credit report may show a balance on those cards. The total balance on your last statement is generally the amount that will show in your credit report.

The amount owed on different types of accounts

In addition to the overall amount you owe, your FICO Scores consider the amount you owe on specific types of accounts, such as credit cards vs. installment loans.

How many accounts have balances?

A larger number of accounts with amounts owed can indicate higher risk of overextension.

Credit utilization ratio on revolving accounts

Your credit utilization ratio on revolving accounts-the percentage of your available credit you're using-is an important factor in your FICO Scores. Using a high percentage of 15 your available credit means you're close to maxing out your credit cards, which can have a negative impact on your FICO Scores.

On the other hand, using a low percentage of your available credit can have a positive impact. *In some cases, a low credit utilization ratio will have a more positive impact on your FICO Scores than not using any of your available credit at all.*

It's also important to note that your current account balance isn't necessarily the balance that shows up on your credit report. Your account balance on your credit report will reflect the account balance your lender reported to the credit bureau (typically the balance from your latest monthly statement), So even if you pay your credit card balances in full each month, your account balance won't necessarily show on your credit report as $0.

How much of the installment loan amounts is still owed, compared with the original loan amount

For example, if you borrowed $10,000 to buy a car and you have paid back $2,000, you still owe (with interest) more than 80% of the original loan. Paying down installment loans is a good sign that you're able and willing to manage and repay debt.

The amounts of debt that you owe is an important part of your credit and makes up 30% of your FICO Score. Keep track of your debt and credit utilization.

Information from www.MyFico.com

Example :

1. The amount owed on all accounts;
Notice the word “ALL.” This means every trade line on the report, good or bad that’s active.

2. The amount owed on different types of accounts; there are only two types of trade lines, which are revolving and installment.

3. How many accounts have balances;
This factor is based on how many trade lines have balances as a whole together.

4. Credit utilization ratio on revolving accounts;
This is your credit limit versus your balance on revolving trade lines only.(credit cards etc.)

5. How much of the installment loan amounts is still owed, compared with the original loan amount; This is your credit limit versus your balance only on your installment loans (student loans, auto loans, signature loans etc.).

To sum up this category of the FICO scoring model, here is an example:

Let's say you have a $3,000 credit limit with a $1,300 balance and a Car Loan at $15,000 and your balance is $5,600.

• Figuring out the Revolving (credit cards) DEBT to CREDIT ratio. The equation is the balance of $1,300 divided by the total credit amount of $3,000. The total DEBT to CREDIT ratio is 43%.

• Figuring out the Installment (car, student loan, signature loan, mortgage etc.) DEBT to ratio. The equation is $5,600 divided by $15,000.
The total DEBT to CREDIT ratio is 37%.

• The equation is the Total balance of $6,900 divided by total credit amount of $18,000. The total DEBT to CREDIT ratio is 38%.

The number you have to constantly move is the Credit Limit Activity, which can be done by sending a $1 check to the credit card companies to keep the activity up to date.

NEVER CLOSE THE SECURED CREDIT CARD

Let's say in January of 2021 you obtained a secured credit card and you add $10,000, but you think you don't need the secured credit card any more. I'd say you should drop it to the bare minimum of $500. Let's say in January of 2025 you need to increase your FICO scores for a purchase. You can increase the secured credit card to the amount you please to make the purchase, since you never closed it and now you have a 4-year aged trade line you can control at your pleasure.

FIRST INCREASE

Date : ______________ Increase Amount : ______________

Score before : ____________ Score After* : ______________

SECOND INCREASE

Date : ______________ Increase Amount : ______________

Score before : ____________ Score After* : ______________

THIRD INCREASE

Date : ______________ Increase Amount : ______________

Score before : ____________ Score After* : ______________

* Please wait 30-45 days to see when the amount invested is posted to Trans Union, Equifax, and Experian.

NOTES

VANCE DOTSON

Founding Partner

Mr. Dotson has been a consumer advocate since 2004 in Oklahoma City, Oklahoma.

He has been a speaker at numerous programs, including the National Consumer Advocates Conferences. Mr. Dotson is focused on helping consumers throughout the country with consumer protection laws mainly dealing with the Fair Credit Reporting Act, Fair Debt Collection Practices Act.

www.ingramcontent.com/pod-product-compliance
Lightning Source LLC
LaVergne TN
LVHW021320160826
845679LV00001B/435

* 9 7 9 8 2 1 8 1 8 6 1 3 5 *